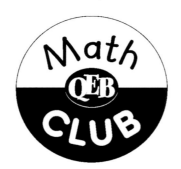

Multiplying

Ann Montague-Smith

QEB Publishing

Published in the United States by
QEB Publishing, Inc
23062 La Cadena Drive
Laguna Hills, CA 92653

www.qeb-publishing.com

Library of Congress Control Number: 2005921278

ISBN 1-59566-114-X

Written by Ann Montague–Smith
Designed and edited by The Complete Works
Illustrated by Peter Lawson
Photography by Steve Lumb

Publisher Steve Evans
Creative Director Louise Morley
Editorial Manager Jean Coppendale

Printed and bound in China

With thanks to:

Contents

Odd and even

Play this game with a friend. You will each need a board game token. Take turns throwing a coin or a third token onto the spinner below. If you land on an odd number, move your token to the first odd number; if even, move to the first even number. Keep taking turns. The first one to reach 30 wins.

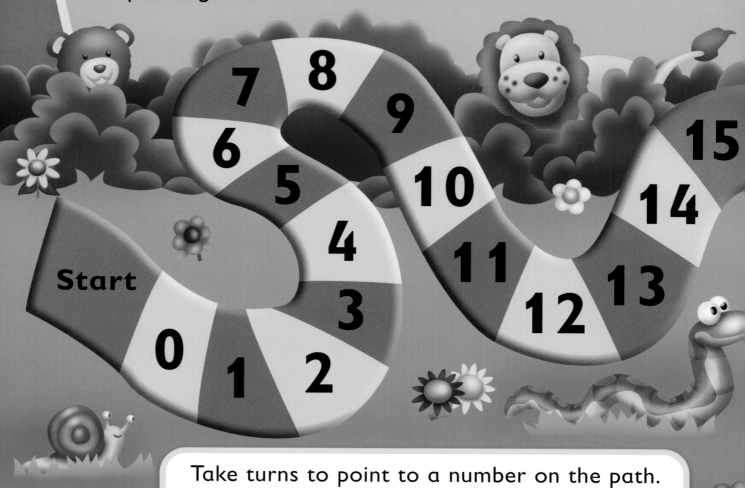

Take turns to point to a number on the path.
Say if it is odd or even.

Now try this

Play the game again.
This time take turns to roll
a 6-sided die. Move your token
the number of spaces shown on the die.
Tell your friend whether the number
you land on is odd or even.

20 21 22 23 24 25 26 27 28 29 30

19 18 17 6

Finish

Spinner
Even
Odd
Odd
Even

5

2s, 3s, 4s, 5s, and 10s

You will need red and blue counters. Count along the row of flowerpots in 2s. Put a red counter on each number you land on. Now count along in 4s and use blue counters. Which numbers have both blue and red counters? What can you say about these numbers?

Start

0 → 1 → 2 → 3 → 4

21 ← 20 ← 19 ← 18 ← 17

22 → 23 → 24 → 25 → 26

6

Do this again for counting in 2s and 3s.

Challenge

Which is the first number that comes in counts of 2s and 3s? Yes, it's 6. Now which is the first number that comes in counts of 2s, 3s, 4s, and 5s? Use a number line if you can't do this in your head.

| 0 | 1 | 2 | 3 | 4 |

5 ➡ 6 ➡ 7 ➡ 8 ➡ 9 ➡ 10

16 ⬅ 15 ⬅ 14 ⬅ 13 ⬅ 12 ⬅ 11

Finish

27 ➡ 28 ➡ 29 ➡ 30 ➡ 31

7

Using arrays

The bees have arranged the cells for their honey in arrays. Look at the array with 8 squares. It is 4 multiplied by 2, or 4x2. It can also be seen as 2x4. Look at the other arrays. Write a multiplication for each array.

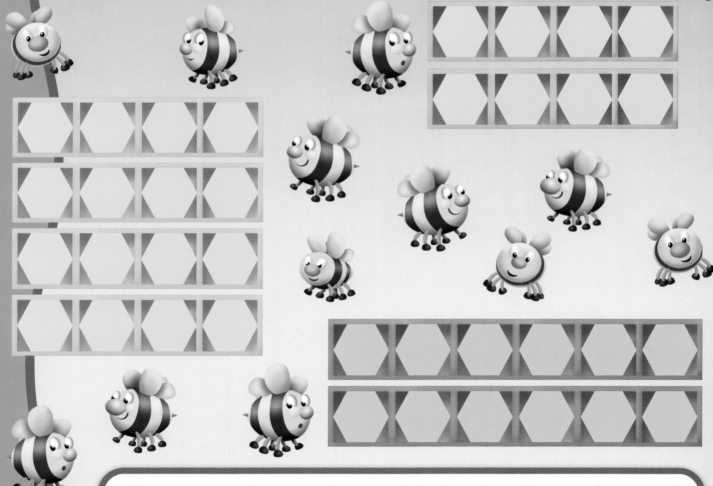

Can you write another multiplication for each array?
Write how many cells there are in each array.

3x2   2x3

9

Doubling

You will need some counters. Choose a number on the sunken boat. Double it. Can you now find the doubled number? If you do, cover both numbers with your counters. If you can't find the double, don't cover any number.

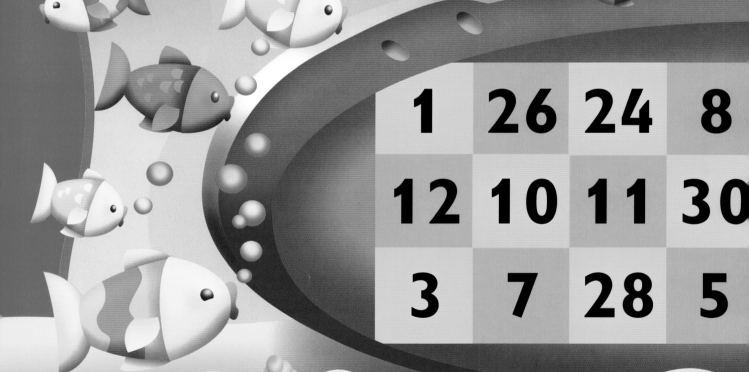

1	26	24	8
12	10	11	30
3	7	28	5

Can you find a way to cover all the numbers on the grid?

Find out

Investigate doubling numbers from 12 to 20. Write down the doubles of these numbers. Tell a friend how you found the answers.

Double 12 is 24.

Double 17 is 34.

4 13 22 2
15 16 6 14
18 20 9

Multiplying by 2s and 10s

Read the multiplication on the card that the boy with blonde hair is holding. Find the answer on a card that a girl is holding.

3x2

18

6x10

90

10x10

5x2

9x10

14

60

7x10

Now match the other problems to the answers.
Which multiplication sentences have an odd answer?

8x2

10

4x10

40

16

Now try this

Think about all the answers to the
questions from the 2 times table.
Is the answer each time odd
or even? Is the answer each time
in the 10 times table odd or even?
Can you think of a reason for your
answers here?

$6 \times 2 = 12$
$3 \times 10 = 30$

6

7x2

9x2

100

70

13

Multiplication for 5s

The bees below are in groups of 5. How many groups are there? So how many bees are there in total? Now look at the butterflies. They are also in groups of 5. Count the groups. How many butterflies are there in total?

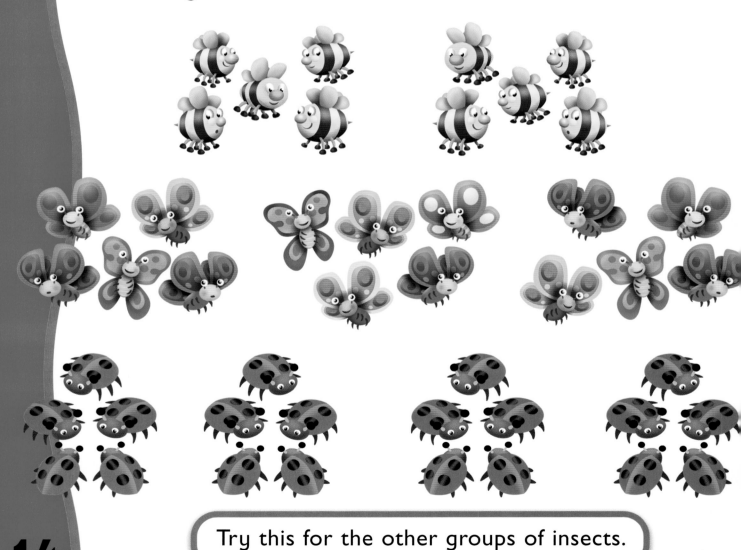

Try this for the other groups of insects.

Now try this

Draw your own groups of insects to show 9x5 and 10x5. Write how many in total there are each time.

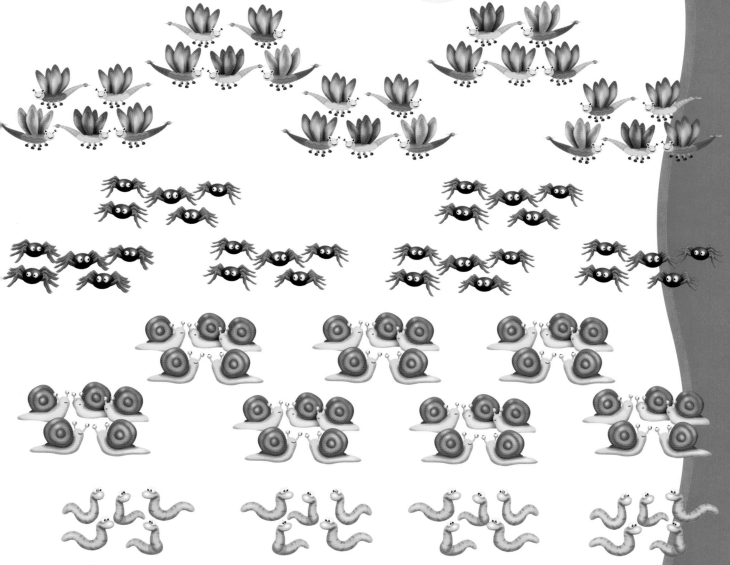

15

More doubles

The wind has blown away the answers to the double questions the animals are holding. Help the animals find the answers.

Which of these doubles are also a multiple of 10?
How can you tell?

80

30

25x2

Try this
Take turns to write down a
number that is in the count of 5,
such as 5, 10, 15. Ask your friend
to say its double. See how quickly
you can do ten of these.

Double 15
is 30.

15

50

100

20x2

45x2

35x2

Number sort

Read the labels on the bags and decide where each number on the right should go. Some numbers can go into more than one bag.

multiples of 2

multiples of 3

multiples of 4

multiples of 5

multiples of 10

One of the numbers does not fit into any of the bags. Can you find it?

6

32

27

12

Challenge

There was one number that would not fit into any of the bags. Think of some more numbers that will not fit. Can you find ten more of them?

11

40

2

30

16

60

45

7

25

9

15

19

Cars and bikes

Look at all the car and bike wheels below.
How many cars do the wheels belong to?
How many bikes do the wheels belong to?

Talk about how you found the answer.

Challenge

Look again at the picture.
Tricycles have three wheels.
How many tricycles could
there be? How many unicycles?

21

Supporting notes

Odd and even, pages 4–5

Count in 2s, from 0 to about 30, and say out loud that these are the even numbers. Repeat, but start on 1, and explain that these are odd numbers. Children can count, jumping with their fingers along the path, to point to the odd or even numbers.

2s, 3s, 4s, 5s, and 10s, pages 6–7

If children count correctly along the rows, they will discover that certain numbers appear in counts of 2s and 4s; for example, 4, 8, and 12. They will also begin to see that the numbers that come in counts of 2s and 5s are the decade numbers, as well as the numbers that come in counts of 10s. Similarly, by comparing counts of 2s and 3s, they will find the multiples of 6: 6, 12, 18, etc. The *Challenge* answer is 60.

Using arrays, pages 8–9

An array is a group of blocks that shows multiplication. Each array can be read in two ways; for example, 3x4 and 4x3. If children are not confident doing this, help them make their own arrays and ask them to count along one side, then along the adjoining side, so that they find the multiplication numbers. They can count all the cells to find the multiplication; for example, 4x3=12.

Doubling, pages 10–11

If children are not confident with doubles of numbers to 15, then use some counters. Count out, say, 12, then another 12, match them to show that there are 2 sets of 12. Now ask the children to count on from 12: 13, 14, 15 … 24 and agree that double 12 is 24.

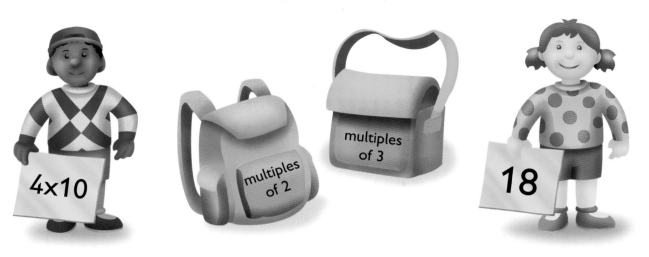

Multiplying by 2s and 10s, pages 12–13

Children need to have rapid recall of the multiplication facts for the 2 and 10 times tables. If they are unsure about an answer, try counting in 2s or 10s, keeping a tally with fingers of how many 2s or 10s have been counted, until the required point in the count has been reached. For example, for 4x2, count 2, 4, 6, 8. So 4x2 is 8.

Multiplication for 5s, pages 14–15

Discourage children from counting each insect one by one. The activity is designed so they should count in 5s: 5, 10, 15, 20, etc. If the children are not confident, then count together in 5s. You could practice counting like this before starting the activity on the page.

More doubles, pages 16–17

This extends children's understanding of doubles to doubles of numbers in the 5 times table. If children are unsure, count up from 0 in 5s to reach the start number. Ask, "How many fives s that? Now count on for the same number of 5s." For example, to find double 20: 5, 10, 15, 20. That is 4 sets of 5. So 25, 30, 35, 40 gives another 4 sets of 5 to reach 40, or double 20.

Number sort, pages 18–19

If children need more help with this activity, use the *2s, 3s, 4s, 5s, and 10s* activity on pages 6 and 7. Now, ask for each number on this page, "Is it a multiple of 2? How can you tell? Is it a multiple of 3 … 4 … ?" Children might find it helpful to count in 2s, 3s, 4s … to check. The odd one out is 7, which is a prime number. Some numbers, such as 16 and 32 (multiples of 2 and 4) and 6 (multiple of 2 and 3) could go into either of the bags.

Cars and bikes, pages 20–21

The children need to count all the car wheels, then all the bicycle wheels. Suggest that they write their totals down on paper. In order to find out how many cars there are, they can count in 4s, and keep a tally on their fingers, until they reach the total of wheels for the cars. For the bicycles, they can count in 2s.

Using this book

The illustrations in this book are bright, cheerful, and colorful, and are designed to capture children's interest. Sit somewhere comfortable together as you look at the book. Children of this age will be able to read most of the instructional words. Help with the reading where necessary, so all children can take part in the activities, regardless of how fluent they are at reading at this point in time.

The activities cover the early concepts associated with multiplication. Children are encouraged to identify odd and even numbers and to count in 2s, 3s, 4s, 5s, and 10s. They learn about arrays, and how these can be read in two ways; for example, an array of 20 blocks in rows of 4s could be seen as 5x4 and 4x5. Children will also extend their knowledge of doubles.

If children are not confident about the multiples of given numbers, encourage them to count in that number. For example, for multiples of 4, for 40, they can count four tens. Encourage them to keep a tally with their fingers to find the multiple. They will begin to realize, like with the arrays, that if they know 4x10=40 then 10x4=40. Over time, children should have rapid recall of the multiplication facts for 2s, 5s, and 10s, and then for 3s and 4s. Learning to recite their multiplication tables is useful, but the practical activities in this book also help children understand the processes involved in multiplication, so the facts and how they are derived make sense.

Encourage children to explain how they found the answers to the questions. Being able to explain their thinking, and to use multiplication vocabulary, helps children clarify in their minds what they are doing. Also, where there are children who are not as confident as others, hearing what the others did, and how they did it, helps them use these methods more effectively.

Encourage children to make notes as they work at an activity. They can record numbers, writing them in order, or write simple sentences to explain. Encourage them to be organized in the way they work, so that they do not miss an important part of the evidence they need to find a solution.

Above all, enjoy the mathematical games, activities, and challenges together.